Anonymous

John Rabone and Sons

Price List: Measuring Rules Measuring Tapes: Spirit Levels

Anonymous

John Rabone and Sons
Price List: Measuring Rules Measuring Tapes: Spirit Levels

ISBN/EAN: 9783337321161

Printed in Europe, USA, Canada, Australia, Japan

Cover: Foto ©Suzi / pixelio.de

More available books at **www.hansebooks.com**

INDEX.

	PAGES.
BEVILS—Boat and Ship Builders' ...	22
Cattle Gauge	51
Dipping Rods for Casks	21
Glasses for Spirit Levels	30
Gauging Rods for Casks	21
Gunter's Navigation Scale	16
LEVELS—Patent Adjusting Plumb	36, 37
Field Sight	32, 33
Masons'	35
Brass	34
Iron ...	34, 35
Plumb ...	32, 33, 36, 37
Surveying ...	33
RULES—Architects'	10, 19
Bench	23
Boxwood, 4-fold ...	3 to 11
„ 2-fold	12 to 17
Brass	14
Brass Bound, 4-fold ...	9
„ „ 2-fold	14, 16
Builders'	10, 19
Calliper Gauge ...	11, 18, 20
Cotton Spinners'	17
Chain Gauge	11
Counter	21, 23
Engine Divided Steel ... „	40, &c.
Engineers' and Smiths' Steel	48, 49

	PAGES.
RULES—Engineers', Carrett's ...	17
„ Cotton Spinners' ...	17
„ Hawthorn's	17
„ Locomotive	17
„ Routledge's ...	17
Glaziers' Laths and T Squares	23
Gauges, various ...	11
„ Chain and Rope	11
Gunter's Navigation Scale ..	16
Iron	14
Ironmongers' ...	11, 20
Ivory ...	18, 19, 20
Parallel	22
Plumb and Level combined ...	35
Saddlers' ...	23
Slide	11, 15, 16 17
Spirit Level combined	14
Shoemakers' ...	21
Steel ...	40 to 49
Tailors' Squares ...	22
TAPES—Spring ...	50, 51
Cattle Gauge	51
Girth ...	58
Metallic Wire ...	53
Linen ..	54, 55
Steel	56, 57
Tailors'	58
Shoe ...	58

PRICE LIST

OF

BOXWOOD, IVORY, BRASS AND STEEL

MEASURING RULES,

ENGINE DIVIDED STEEL STRAIGHT EDGES,

MEASURING TAPES,

WITH

METALLIC WIRE, STEEL, & LINEN TAPES,

BRASS, IRON, AND WOOD

SPIRIT LEVELS, &c.,

MANUFACTURED BY

JOHN RABONE & SONS,

(ESTABLISHED 1784),

TRADE MARK.

HOCKLEY ABBEY

TRADE MARK.

HOCKLEY ABBEY

HOCKLEY ABBEY WORKS,

BIRMINGHAM.

ORDERS EXECUTED ONLY THROUGH MERCHANTS AND FACTORS.

Entered at Stationers' Hall.

July, 1878.

HOCKLEY ABBEY WORKS,

BIRMINGHAM, July, 1878.

GENTLEMEN,

In issuing a New Edition of the Price List of the various articles manufactured by us, we have pleasure in pointing out to your notice that it is much more complete, and is better classified and arranged, than any heretofore presented. It has undergone an entire revision : A GREAT REDUCTION HAS BEEN MADE IN THE PRICES of many of the articles, *and in no case have any been increased.* This we have been enabled to do by the progressive improvements in our machinery, and the adaptation of the same to some of those processes, which till now have been effected by uncertain, and at the best, expensive hand labour.

The BOXWOOD RULES will all be found to be made of well-seasoned Boxwood of good quality, proportioned to the prices ; and instead of having only a few inches divided into sixteenths, as those usually made in the trade, they are marked outside in eighths, and inside in sixteenths the whole length of the rule.

The ENGINE DIVIDED STEEL RULES (pages 40, &c.) are especially recommended for the fineness and accuracy of their graduation, being marked from $\frac{1}{8}$ths to $\frac{1}{64}$ths of an inch, and are invaluable to Engineers, Machinists, and to all who require great exactness. The other Steel Rules (pages 48, 49) for Smiths' use, will be found to be superior to those usually made.

The STEEL MEASURING TAPES, and the METALLIC WIRED TAPES, will be found of superior quality, being marked by the most modern and approved methods.

In conclusion : Our aim will be, as it has been, to adopt every improvement in machinery, or otherwise, and to still progress and excel in the quality of all goods manufactured by us ; and whenever reductions in prices of materials, or other means enable us, we shall offer to our friends, as we have hitherto done, every advantage in our power, and thus afford them greater inducements and facilities for the disposal of our goods with mutual credit and advantage.

Yours truly,

JOHN RABONE & SONS.

In ordering Rules *it is sufficient* to quote numbers and length, thus No 1155   2 Feet.

If no **FOREIGN MEASURES** are specified in order, the goods will be sent English measure.

Box Rules are supplied 2-**FEET ENGLISH AND FRENCH MILLIMETRES** at List Prices.
If required one metre long, they are charged 6d. to 2/- per dozen extra to 3 feet List Prices.
(excepting a few expensive patterns.)

Rules marked with **THREE MEASURES** are charged 1/- to 2/- per dozen extra to List Prices.

All Rules may be had with any **FOREIGN MEASURES** to order.

Two Feet, Four Fold Boxwood Rules.

EXTRA THICK.

Packed in Dozens in Paper Boxes

			2 feet.	3 feet.
No. 2325.	Round Joint, Extra Thick	¾ inch wide	6/-	8/- per dozen
,, 2326.	,, ,, ,,	⅞ inch wide	5/-	7/- ,,
,, 2329.	,, ,, ,,	1 inch wide	6/9	9/- ,,
,, 2333.	Square Joint	1 inch wide	10/-	13/- ,,
,, 2334.	Round Joint	1¼ inch wide	8/6	—

No. 2325.

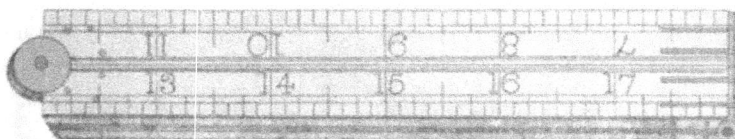

No. 2329.

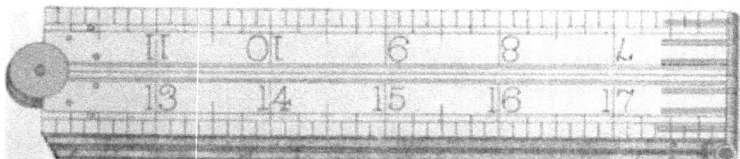

No. 2334.

One Foot, Four Fold Boxwood Rules.

MARKED INCHES IN 8ths & 16ths. FRENCH POLISHED.

Packed in Dozens in Paper Boxes.

				1 foot.
No. 2320.	Round Joint,		⅜ inch wide	5/6 per dozen
„ 2321.	Square Joint,	...	⅝ inch wide	7/– „
„ 2322.	Arch Joint,	...	¾ inch wide	9/–
„ 2324.	Arch Joint, Edge Plates, ...	„ „	12/–

No. 2320.

No. 2321.

No. 2322.

No. 2324.

Two Feet, Four Fold Boxwood Rules.

MARKED INCHES IN 8ths & 16ths. FRENCH POLISHED.

Packed in Dozens in Paper Boxes.

				2 feet.	3 feet.
No. 2336.	Round Joint,		1 inch wide	7/–	9/6 per dozen
„ 2339.	Square Joint,	... ...	1 inch wide	8/6	11/– „
„ 2338.	„ „ Ex. Strong Small Joints.	... ...	10/–	13/– „

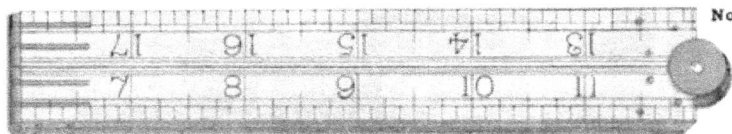

No. 2336.

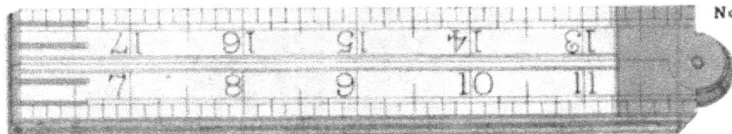

No. 2339.

FULL SIZE DRAWINGS.

Two Feet, Four Fold Boxwood Rules,

FRENCH POLISHED.

Packed in Dozens in Paper Boxes.

No.								2 feet.	3 feet.	
No. 2545.	Arch Joint, Inches in 8ths, 16ths and 10ths					1 inch wide		10/-	12/-	per dozen
„ 2546.		„	„	„		1 inch wide		11/-	13/6	„
„ 2547.	„	„	„	„	„	1¼ inch wide		12/6	15/6	„
„ 2548.	„	„	„	„	„	1½ inch wide		14/6	17/6	„
„ 2549.	„	Inches in 8ths, 16ths and Scales				1½ inch wide	...	16/6	20/-	„

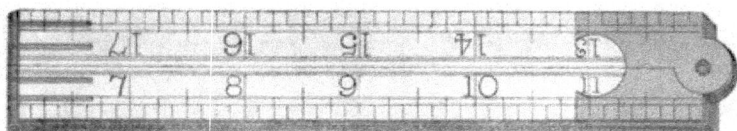

No. 2545.

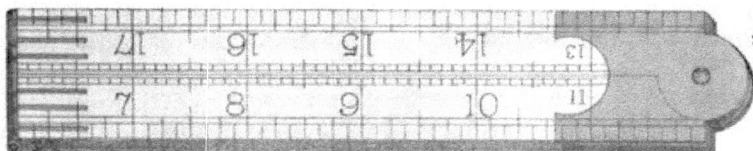

No. 2547.

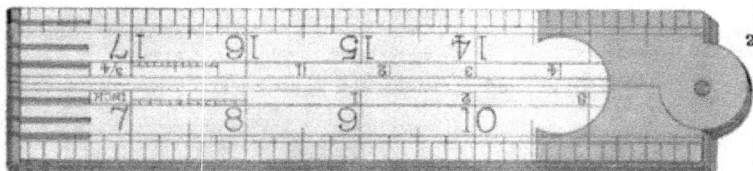

No. 2548.

Two Feet, Four Fold Boxwood Rules,

MARKED INCHES IN 8ths & 16ths.　FRENCH POLISHED.

Packed in Half-Dozens in Paper Boxes.

										2 feet.	3 feet.	
No. **2341**.	Arch Joint, Ex. Strong Small Joints, Brass Pin Holes							$\frac{3}{4}$ inch wide	14/-	17/- per dozen.
,, **2344**.	,,	,,	,,	,,	,,	,,	1 inch wide	14/-	17/-	,,
,, **2349**.	,,	,,	,,	,,	,,	,,	1$\frac{1}{8}$ inch wide	16/-	19/-	,,
,, **2352**.	,,	,,	,,	,,	,,	,,	1$\frac{1}{4}$ inch wide	18/-	21/-	,,
,, **2355**.	,,	,,	,,	,,	,,	,,	1$\frac{1}{2}$ inch wide	20/-	23/-	,,
,, **2357**.	Engraved Arch Joint, Ex. Strong Small Joints, Brass Pin Holes							1$\frac{1}{2}$ inch wide	24/-	27/-	,,

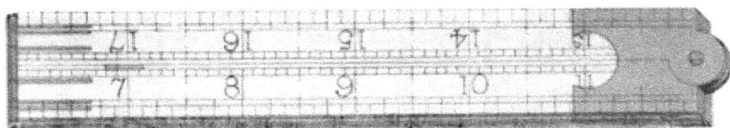

No. 2344.

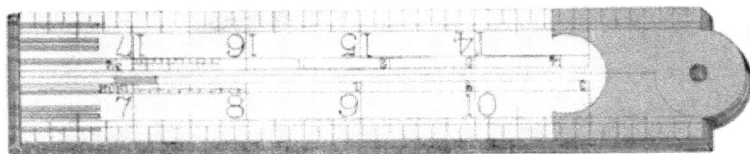

No. 2349.

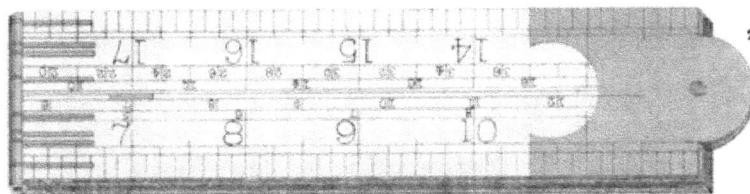

No. 2355.

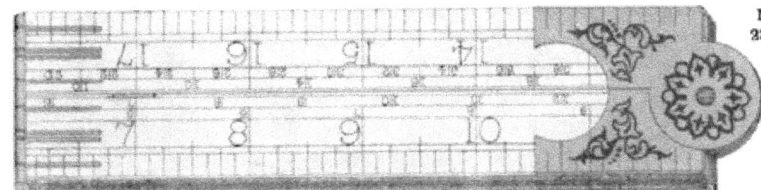

No. 2357.

Two Feet, Four Fold Boxwood Rules,

Marked Inches in 8ths & 16ths.   French Polished.

Packed in Half-Dozens in Paper Boxes.

The Small-Joints of these Rules are of a new description, *both the edge-plates and the middle-plates forming part of the hinge of the Joint* thus giving the Rule a strength, durability and style never before attained.

												2 feet.	3 feet.	
No 2342	Arch Joints, Edge-plates, Inches in 8ths, 16ths, 10ths and 12ths							...		½ inch wide	20/-	23/- per doz
,, 2345	,,	,,	,,	,,	,,	,,	,,	,,		1 inch wide	20/-	23/-	,,
,, 2350	,,			,,	,,	,,	,,	& Scales	1¼ inch wide	22/-	25/-	,,
,, 1110				,,	,,	,,	,,	,,	1½ inch wide	23/-	26/-	
, 2358				,,	,,	,,	,,	,,	1½ inch wide	25/-	28/-	

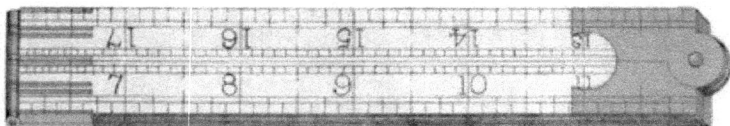

No 2345

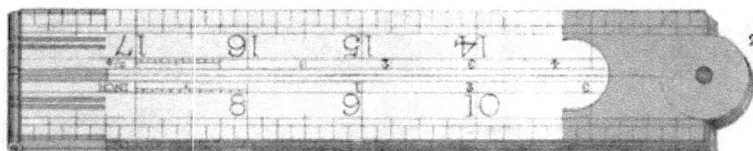

No. 2350

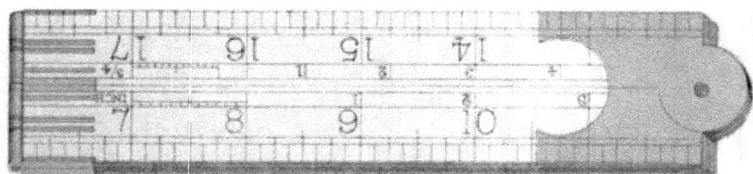

No 1110

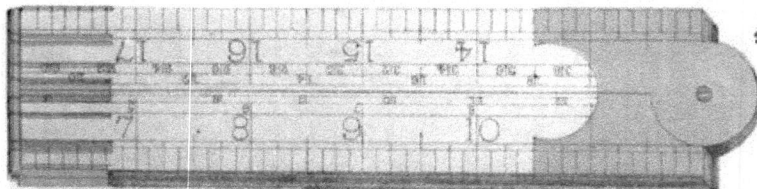

No 2358

Two Feet, Four Fold Boxwood Rules,

MARKED INCHES IN 8ths, 16ths, 10ths and 12ths. FRENCH POLISHED.

Packed in Half-Dozens in Paper Boxes.

								2 feet.	3 feet.	
No. **2361**.	Double Arch Joint, Brass Pin Holes	...	...				⅜ inch wide	22/-	25/- per dozn.	
,, **2362**.	,,	,,	,,	,,	...	...	1 inch wide	22/-	25/-	,,
,, **2363**.	,,	,,	,,	,,	and Scales	...	1¼ inch wide	24/-	27/-	,,
,, **2364**.	,,	,,	,,	,,	,,	...	1⅜ inch wide	26/-	29/-	,,
,, **2365**.	,,	,,	,,	,,	,,	...	1½ inch wide	28/-	31/-	,,
,, **2366**.	,,	,,	Brass Bound Edges	,,		...	1⅝ inch wide	48/-	66/-	,,

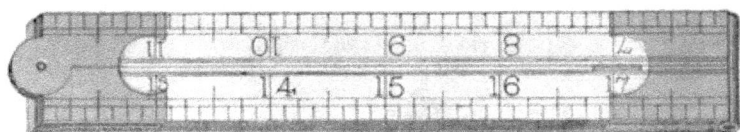

No. 2362.

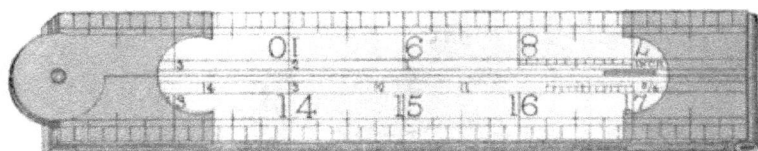

No. 2363.

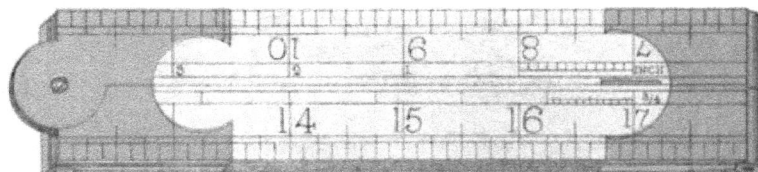

No. 2364.

Two Feet, Four Fold Boxwood Rules,

MARKED INCHES IN 8ths, 16ths, 10ths and 12ths. FRENCH POLISHED.

WITH ARCH JOINTS & BRASS BOUND EDGES.

Packed in Half-Dozens in Paper Boxes.

								2 feet.	3 feet.
No. 1112.	Arch Joint, Outside Edges Brass Bound				...	...	1½ inch wide	23/–	36/– per dozen.
„ 1113.	„	„	„	„	...	...	1¼ inch wide	28/–	42/– „
„ 1114.	„	„	„	„	...	...	1⅛ inch wide	33/–	48/– „
„ 1115.	„	Outside and Inside Edges Brass Bound			...		1½ inch wide	30/–	50/– „
„ 1116.	„	„	„	„	„	...	1¼ inch wide	36/–	56/– „
„ 1117.	„	„	„	„	„	...	1⅛ inch wide	42/–	65/– „

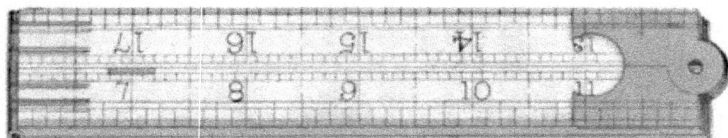

No. 1112.

Two Feet, Four Fold Boxwood Rules,

MARKED INCHES IN 8ths, 16ths, 10ths, and 12ths.

The Inside Edges of these Rules are Bevilled and marked with various Drawing Scales, and are much esteemed by Architects, Builders, Carpenters, and all who draw or work from plans.

Packed in Half-Dozens in Paper Boxes.

											2 feet.	3 feet.
No. 1118.	Arch Joint, Bevilled Edges with 8 Scales					...	...	...	1 inch wide	22/-	30/- per dozen.
,, 1119.	,, Edge-plates, Bevilled Edges with 8 Scales						...	...	1¼ inch wide	30/-	39/-	,,
,, 1120.	,,	,,	,,	,,	,,	,,	...	...	1½ inch wide	36/-	45/-	,,
,, 1121.	,,	G.S. Mounts	,,	,,	,,	,,	...	...	1 inch wide	42/-	54/-	,,
,, 1122.	,,	,,	,,	,,	,,	16 Scales, Angles on Joints	1½ inch wide	54/-	66/-	,,
,, 1123.	,, and Edge-plates	,,	,,	,,	,,	,,	,,	...	1½ inch wide	66/-	78/-	,,

Half size Drawings.

No. 1118.

No. 1119.

No. 1120.

No. 1121.

GERMAN SILVER MOUNTS.

No. 1122.

GERMAN SILVER MOUNTS.

No. 1123.

GERMAN SILVER MOUNTS.

HALF SIZE DRAWINGS.

Boxwood Rules, with Slides and Calliper Gauges.
Half Size Drawings.

Boxwood Rope and Chain Gauge,
2 inches wide.

4 inch long, **No. 2376.** 26/- per dozen.
6 inch long, **No. 2377.** 32/-   ,,

Two Feet, Four Fold Boxwood Rule, Brass Slide.
1½ inch wide.

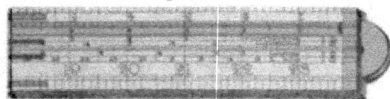

No. 2378. 28/- per dozen

Two Feet Four Fold Boxwood Rule, Brass Slide.
1½ inch wide.

No. 2379. 39/- per dozen.

One Foot, Four Fold Boxwood Rule, Calliper Gauge
1 inch wide.

No. 2381. 28/- per dozen

Two Feet, Four Fold Box Slide Rule.
1½ inch wide.

No. 2380. 36/- per dozen

Two Feet, Four Fold Calliper Gauge Rule.   1½ inch wide.

No. 2382. 46/- per dozen.

Two Feet Four Fold Ironmongers' Rule, or Iron Gauge.   1½ inch wide.

No. 2383. 54/- per dozen.

One Foot, Three Fold Ironmongers' Rule or Iron Gauge.   1½ inch wide.

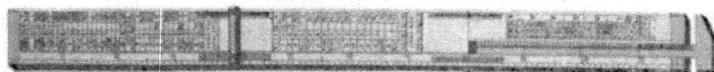

No. 2384. 36/- per dozen.

Two Feet, Two Fold Boxwood Rules,

MARKED INCHES IN 8ths, and 16ths.

Packed in Dozens in Paper Boxes.

No. 2386.	Round Joint, Thick Rule, Inches in 8ths	...	...	...	...	1½ inch wide	4/6 per dozen.
" " 2388.	Square Joint, Inches in 8ths	...	...	...	...	1½ inch wide	6/6 "
" 2387.	" " " and 8 Square Line	...	...	...	" "	7/9 "
" 2389.	A Joint, Inches in 8ths and 16ths, and 8 Square Line	...	...	...	" "	8/6 "
" 2390.	" " " " " and Scales Polished	...	...	" "	10/6 "
" 2391.	" " " " " " Bevilled Edge, Polished	" "	11/6 "
" 1124.	Arch Joint, Inches in 8ths and 16ths, 8 Square Line	...	...	" "	9/3 "
" 2394.	" " " " " Scales, Bevilled Edge, Polished	...	" "	10/- "

Half size Drawings.

No. 2386.

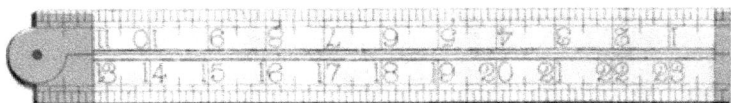

No. 2387.

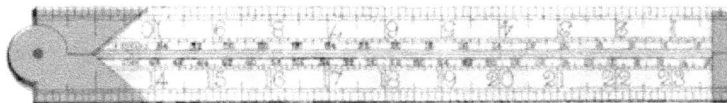

No. 2389.

No. 2390.

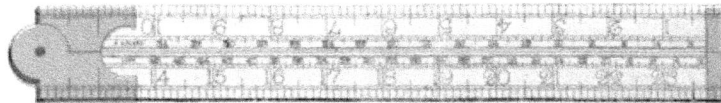

No. 1124.

No. 2394.

Two Feet, Two Fold Boxwood Rules,

MARKED INCHES IN 8ths and 16ths. FRENCH POLISHED.

All 1¼ inch wide.   *Packed in Dozens in Paper Boxes.*

No. 2393.	Arch Joint, Brass Pin Holes, 8 Square Line and Scales	...	...	...	...	11/6	per dozen.
,, 2398.	,, ,, ,, ,, ,, ,, Bevilled Edge ...					13/-	,,
,, 2395.	,, ,, ,, ,, ,, ,, ,, ,, ,, ...					15/-	,,
,, 2396.	,, ,, ,, ,, ,, ,, Double Bevilled Edges					17/-	,,
,, 2400.	Vulcan Joint, ,, ,, ,, ,, ,, Bevilled Edge ...					16/-	,,
,, 2401.	Atlas Joint, ,, ,, ,, ,, ,, ,, ,, ,, ...					16/-	,,
,, 2402.	Vulcan Joint ,, ,, ,, ,, ,, Double Bevilled Edges					19/-	,,
,, 2399.	Waterloo Joint ,, ,, ,, ,, ...					20/-	,,
,, 2404.	Engraved Arch Joint, 8 Square line and Scales, Bevilled Edge					12/-	,,
,, 2405.	,, ,, ,, Brass Pin Holes, 8 Square Line and Scales, Bevilled Edges					16/-	,,
,, 2406.	,, ,, ,, ,, ,, ,, ,, ,, Double Bevilled Edge					20/-	,,

Half Size Drawings.

No. 2393.

No. 2398.

No. 2400.

No. 2401.

No. 2402.

No. 2404.

Two Feet, Two Fold Boxwood Rules,

Marked Inches in 8ths, and 16ths.   French Polished.

All 1½ inch wide.   *Packed in Dozens in Paper Boxes.*

No. 2407.	Arch Joint. Brass Bound Edges ...	...	...	...	24/- per dozen.
" 2410.	Grecian Joint, Extra Thin Rule, Bevilled Edge	...	...	20/-	"
" 2411.	Arch Joint, Spirit Level, and Degrees on Joint	...	...	36/-	"
" 2412.	" " " " " with Brass Slide	...	48/-	"
" 2360.	Two feet, four fold Rule, Spirit Level, and Degrees on Joint	...	...	48/-	"

Half size Drawings.

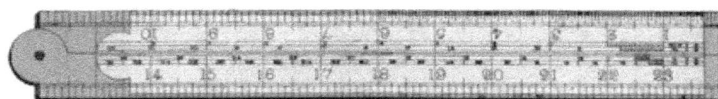

No. 2407.

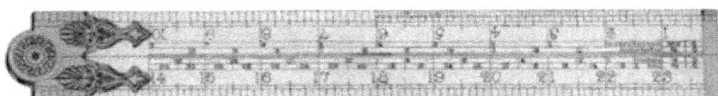

No. 2410.

No. 2411.

Two Feet, Two Fold, Brass and Iron Rules.

No. 3413.	Flexible Brass Rule Round Joint	¾ inch wide	8/6 per dozen.
" 1125.	" "	⅞ inch wide	11/6 "
" 3414.	" " Grecian Joint	1⅛ inch wide	18/6 "
" 3415.	Two feet, two fold Iron Rule	" "	6/- "

No. 2413.

No. 2414.

No. 2415.

HALF SIZE DRAWINGS.

Two Feet, Two Fold Boxwood Rules,

MARKED INCHES IN 8ths and 16ths.

BRASS SLIDES. FRENCH POLISHED.

All 1½ inch wide. *Packed in Half-Dozens in Paper Boxes.*

No.											
No. 2416.	Arch Joint, Slide marked Inches in 16ths	...	...	...			17/- per dozen
„ **2417.**	„	„	„	„	„	Bevilled Edge	...			19/-	„
„ **1126.**	„	„	„	„	„	and Gunter's Line, Bevilled Edge	22/-	„
„ **2418.**	„	„	„	„	„	„	„	„	„	25/-	„
„ **1127.**	„	„	„	„	„	„	„	„	„	28/-	„
„ **2420.**	Vulcan Joint	„	„	„	„	Bevilled Edge	...			24/-	„
„ **2421.**	„	„	„	„	„	and Gunter's Line, Bevilled Edge	27/-	„
„ **2423.**	„	„	„	„	„	„	„	„	„	30;-	„

Books of Instructions for "THE SLIDE RULE," by J. RABONE & SONS, 2/6 per dozen subject.

Half size Drawings.

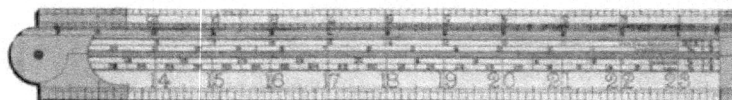

No. 2417.

No. 2418.

No. 1127.

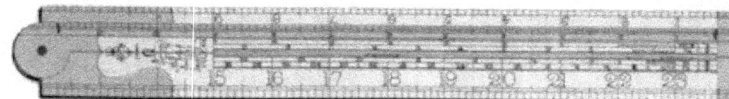

No. 2420.

No. 2421

No. 2423.

HALF SIZE DRAWINGS.

Two Feet, Two Fold Boxwood Rules,

MARKED INCHES IN 8ths, and 16ths.

BRASS SLIDES. FRENCH POLISHED.

All 1⅜ inch wide. *Packed in Half-Dozens in Paper Boxes.*

No. 2425.	Arch Joint, Brass Slide, Brass Bound Edges	36/- per dozen.
.. 2426.	.. .. and Bevilled Edges	46/- ..
.. 2424.	.. Ivory Slide Bevilled Edge	51/- ..
.. 1128.	.. Brass Slide, Tables for Timber Measuring	30/- ..
.. 1129.	2 feet, 3 fold Rule, Ivory Slide, Tables for Timber Measuring	68/- ..

Books of Instructions for "THE SLIDE RULE," *by J. RABONE & SONS, 2/6 per dozen subject.*

Half size Drawings.

No. 2425.

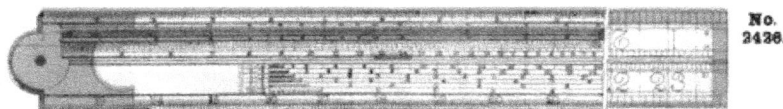

No. 2426.

No. 2424.

Boxwood Gunter's Navigation Scales.

No. 2427. 12 inch, 14/- 24 inch, 20/- per dozen.

Engineers' Boxwood Rules.

All 1¾ inch wide.

No. 2428	Two feet, two fold Routledge's Engineers' Rule	...	...	...	38/- per dozen
„ 2429.	„ „ „ „ „ Brass-bound Edges	...			58/- „
„ 2430.	Two feet, four fold Routledge's Engineers' Rule			...	56/- „
„ 2431.	Two feet, two fold Carrett's Engineers' Rule...	...	...	...	56/- „
„ 2432.	„ „ Hawthorn's Locomotive Engineers' Rule			...	56/- „

Books of Instructions for above, 4/- per dozen.

„ 2433.	Two feet, two fold Slater's Cotton Spinners' Rule	...		...	82/- „
„ 1130	„ „ Wilkinson's, Routledge's Engineers' Rule	...		...	56/- „
„ 1131	„ „ „ „ „ Brass Edges			...	72/- „

Half size Drawings.

No. 2428.

No. 2430.

No. 2431.

No. 2432.

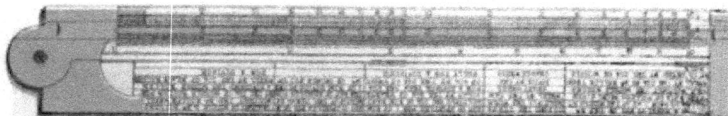

No. 2433

One Foot, Four Fold Ivory Rules.

No. 2435.	Round Joint, Brass Mounts			½ inch wide.	24/6 per doz.
,, 2436.	,,	,,	,,	,, ,, ,,	20/- ,,
,, 2437.	Square Joint	,,	,,	,, ,, ,,	37/- ,,
,, 2438.	,,	G. S. Mounts		,, ,, ,,	43/- ,,
,, 2439.	Round Joint, Brass Mounts			⅝ inch wide.	42/- ,,
,, 2440.	Arch Joint, G.S. Mounts			,, ,, ,,	69/- ,,
,, 2441.	,,	Edge Plates, G. S. Mounts		,, ,, ,,	92/- ,,
,, 2442.	,,	G. S. Mounts, Calliper Gauge		,, ,, ,,	10/6 each.
,, 2443.	,,	,,	,,	1 inch wide.	9/- each.
,, 2444.	,,	,,	,, Calliper Gauge	,, ,, ,,	14/- each.
,, 2445.	,,	,,	,, and Iron Tables ...	1¼ inch wide.	17/6 each.
,, 2446.	One foot, three fold Ironmongers' Rule, G. S. Mounts, Calliper Gauge and Iron Tables			,, ,, ,,	20/6 each.
,, 2434.	Six inch, two fold Ivory Rule, Brass Mounts ...			½ inch wide.	10/- per doz.

Full size Drawings.

No. 2435.

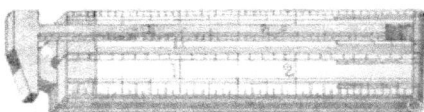

No. 2442.

No. 2437.

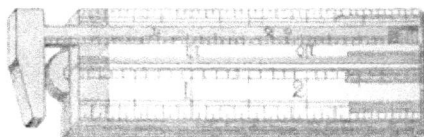

No. 2440.

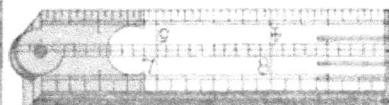

No. 2444.

No. 2443.

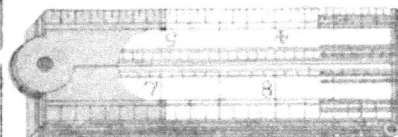

No. 2445.

No. 2446.

FULL SIZE DRAWINGS.

Two Feet, Four Fold Ivory Rules.

No. 2448	Round Joint, Brass Mounts			½ inch wide	5/- each
„ 2449	„	„	„	¾ inch wide	8/6 „
„ 2450	Arch Joint, G S Mounts		„ „ „		10/6 „
„ 2451	„	Edge Plates, G S Mounts	„ „ „		12/- „
„ 2452	„	G S Mounts		1 inch wide	13/6 „
„ 2454	„	„		1¼ inch wide	17/- „
„ 2455	„	Edge Plates, G S Mounts	„ „		18/6
„ 2456	„	G S Mounts		1½ inch wide	23/- „

With Inside Edges Bevilled, and marked with Drawing Scales for Architects', Builders', Surveyors' and others.

No. 2458	With 8 Scales	1 inch wide	17/- each.
„ 2459	With 16 Scales and Angles on Joint	1½ inch wide	20/- „

Full size Drawings.

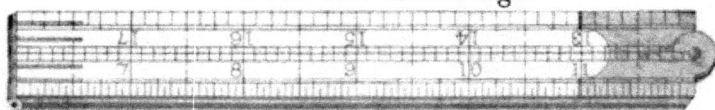

No. 2450.

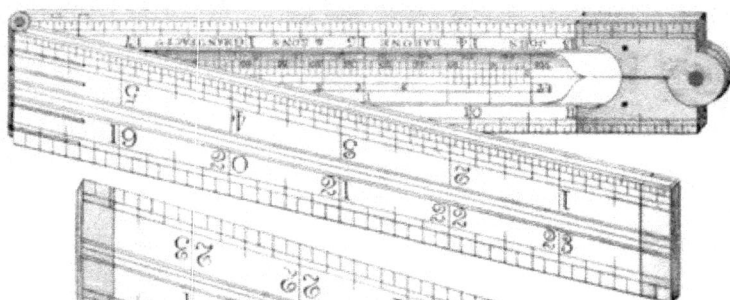

No. 2458.

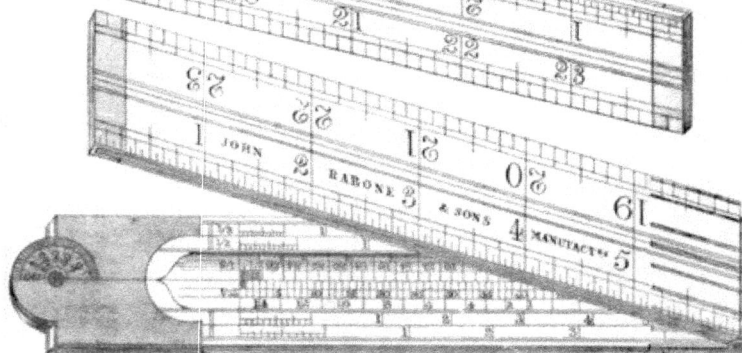

No. 2459.

Two Feet, Four Fold Ivory Rules.

WITH SLIDES & CALLIPER GAUGES.

No. 2453	Arch Joint, Calliper Gauge, G. S. Mounts	1 inch wide.	18/6 each.
,, 2447	Arch Joint, Calliper Gauge, Iron and Copper Tables, for Ironmongers' use	1¼ inch wide.	23/- ,,
,, 2457	Routledge's Engineers' Rule, Arch Joint, G. S. Mounts, Slide, and Engineers' Table	1¼ inch wide.	31/- ,,

Full size Drawings.

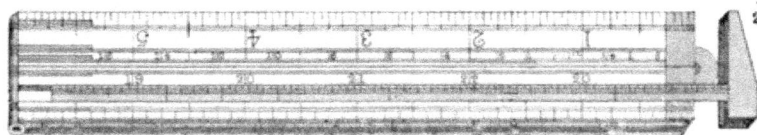

No. 2453.

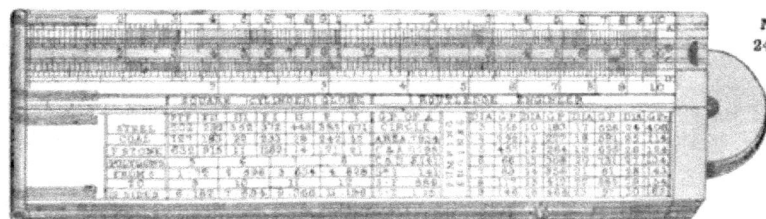

No. 2457.

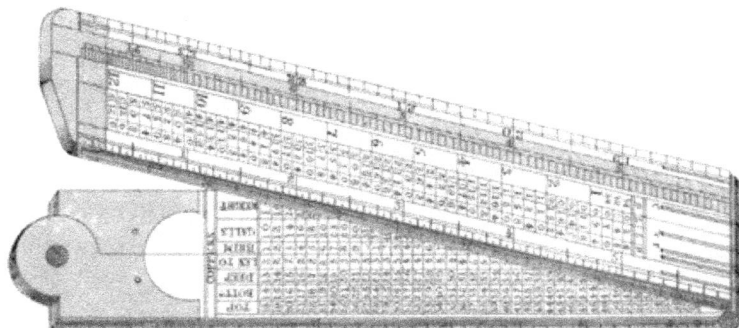

No. 2447

FULL SIZE DRAWINGS.

Shoemakers' Size Sticks.

No. 2478.	Folding Size Stick, Brass Feet, Inches and Shoe Sizes						...	$\frac{7}{16}$ inch wide.	9/- per dozen.	
,, 2479.	,,	,,	,,	,,	,,	,,	,,	$\frac{1}{2}$ inch wide.	11/6	,,
,, 2480.	,,	,,	,,	,,	,,	,,	...	$\frac{9}{16}$ inch wide.	14/-	,,
,, 2481.	,,	,,	,,	Wood Feet	,,	,,	...	1 inch wide.	17/6	,,
,, 1133.	,,	,,	,,	,,	,,	,,	...	$\frac{3}{4}$ inch wide.	15/6	,,
,, 2482.	Size Stick to fold to 6 Inches, with Feet to fold inside						...	1 inch wide.	18/-	,,
,, 1133.	Straight Counter size Stick ...		...				...	$\frac{3}{4}$ inch wide.	15/6	,,

Half size Drawings.

No. 2478.

No. 2481.

Gauging Rods.

No. 1134.	Four feet Gauging Rod, Brass Tipped, Imperial Gallons ...				...		...	...	32/- per dozen.	
,, 2483.	,,	,,	,,	,,	,,	,,	and Tables of Outs	...	42/-	,,
,, 2484.	,,	,,	,,	,,	,,	Imperial and Old Wine Gallons and				
	Imperial Tables of Outs			...	...	...		...	54/-	,,

No. 2483.

No. 2484.

Brass Counter Measures,
FOR SCREWING DOWN ON COUNTERS.

No. 2485.	Three feet Counter measure, marked Nails ...				...		$\frac{3}{4}$ inch wide.	20/- per doz.		
,, 2486.	,,	,,	,,	,,	Inches ...	...	...	,, ,, ,,	25/-	,,
,, 2487.	,,	,,	,,	,,	Inches and Nails	...		1 inch wide.	33/-	,,
,, 2488.	1 Metre	,,	,,	,,	in Half Centimetres ...			$\frac{3}{4}$ inch wide.	30/-	,,
,, 2489.	,,	,,	,,	,,	,,	,,				
	and English Inches ...			...	...	...		1 inch wide.	40/-	,,

Boat Builders' Bevils.

No. 2491.	12 inch Rosewood Bevils, Two Brass Tongues							10/- per dozen
,, 2492.	,,	,,	,,	,,	,,	,,	extra strong	14.-
,, 1135.		Boxwood	,,			,,	marked inches in 8ths	10/-
,, 2493.					,,	,,	extra strong, marked Inches in 8ths	16/-

Half size Drawings.

No.
2492.

No.
2493.

Boxwood Tailors' Square.

WITH BRASS JOINT TO FOLD. 2 INCH WIDE WHEN CLOSED.

No 2494.	
18 in.	33/- per dozen.
21 in.	36/- ,,
24 in.	39/- ,,
27 in.	42/- ,,

Ebony Parallel Rule.

Laths and Bench Rules.

GLAZIERS' THIN LATHS.   BRASS TIPPED.

1¾ inch Wide.   ¼ inch Thick.   MARKED IN INCHES.

13/-	17/-	21/- per dozen.
No. 1136. 24 inch.	30 inch.	36 inch.

GLAZIERS' T SQUARES.   BRASS TIPPED.

MARKED IN INCHES.

21/-	25/-	28/- per dozen.
No. 1137. 24 inch.	30 inch.	36/- inch.

Straight Bench Rules,

BRASS TIPPED.   MARKED IN INCHES.

			2 feet	3 feet	4 feet	5 feet	6 feet	
1 inch Wide	⁵⁄₁₆ inch Thick	**No. 1138.**	12/-	15/-	--	—	—	per dozen.
1¼ inch Wide	¼ inch Thick	**No. 1139.**	—	18/6	27/-	45/-	—	
EXTRA STRONG. 2 inch Wide	⅜ inch Thick	**No. 1140.**	—	27/-	42/-	54/-	72/-	

Boxwood Saddlers' Rules,

BEVILLED EDGE.   MARKED IN INCHES.

			2 feet	3 feet	
2 inch Wide	⅜ inch Thick	**No. 1141.**	36/-	54/-	per dozen.

Drapers' Round Yard Sticks.

Common Marked with Nails	...	**No. 1142.**	3/- per dozen.
Lancewood Marked with Inches and Nails		**No. 1143.**	9/- ,,

Best Proved Spirit Level Tubes.

1½ inch	2/6 per dozen.	3 inch	4/- per dozen.	4½ inch	6/- per dozen.
2 ,,	3/- ,,	3½ ,,	4/6 ,,	5 ,,	7/- ,,
2½ ,,	3/6 ,,	4 ,,	5/- ,,	6 ,,	12/- ,,

Warranted Spirit Levels,

FRENCH POLISHED.   WITH BEST PROVED TUBES.

Half size Drawings.

BRASS PLATED LEVEL.
No. 2496.

		6in.	8in.	9in.	10in.	12in.
Brass Plated Top	No. 2496.	9/3	12/6	14/-	15/6	18/6 per dozen.
Brass Plated Top and Bottom ...	,, 2496.	18/-	23/-	26/-	30/-	36/- ,,

BRASS PLATED LEVEL,
TIPPED BOTTOM.
No. 2500.

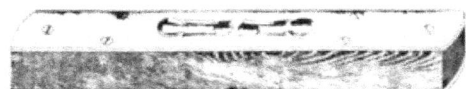

		8in.	9in.	10in.	12in.	14in.
Brass Plated Top	No. 2499.	18/-	20/-	23/-	28/-	32/- per dozen.
Brass Plated Top and Tipped Bottom	,, 2500.	23/-	25/-	27/-	33/-	37/- ,,
Brass Plated Top and Bottom ...	,, 2501.	30/-	33/-	37/-	44/-	53/- ,,

BEST SPIRIT LEVEL.
BRASS PLATED TOP & BOTTOM.
No. 2506.

		8in.	9in.	10in.	12in.	14in.	16in.	18in.	20in.	24in.
Brass Plated Top and Tipped Bottom	No. 2505.	28/-	30/-	32/-	37/-	41/-	50/-	62/-	74/-	103/- per doz
Brass Plated Top and Bottom ...	,, 2506.	34/-	38/-	42/-	48/-	58/-	70/-	84/-	100/-	138/- ,,

HALF SIZE DRAWINGS.

Warranted Spirit Levels.

FRENCH POLISHED.   WITH BEST PROVED TUBES.

Half size Drawings.

EXTRA WIDE ROSEWOOD BRASS PLATED LEVEL.

No. 2502.

				8in.	9in.	10in.	12in.	14in.	18in.
Brass Plated Top	...	...	No. 2502.	30/-	33/-	36/-	40/-	51 -	70/- per dozen.
,, ,, ,,	and Bottom		,, 2503.	40/-	45/-	49/-	56/-	68/-	100/- ,,

EXTRA WIDE EBONY BRASS PLATED LEVEL.

No. 2514.

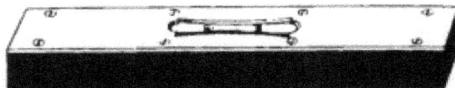

				8in.	9in.	10in.	12in.
Brass Plated Top	...	...	No. 2514.	34/-	38/-	42/-	50/- per dozen.
,, ,, ,,	and Bottom...		,, 2515.	48/-	53/-	58/-	68/- ,,

EXTRA SMALL ROSEWOOD LEVEL.

No. 2507.

			6in.	8in.	9in.	10in.	12in.
Brass Plated Top and Tipped Bottom ...	No. 2507.	18/-	23/-	27/-	30/-	36/- per dozen.
Raised Brass Top and Tipped Bottom ...	,, 2508.	—	27/-	30/-	33/-	40/- ,,
Ebony Level, Plated Top and Tipped ...	,, 2511.	—	28/-	32/-	36/-	40/- ,,

EXTRA SMALL ROSEWOOD LEVEL.

		8in.	9in.	10in.	12in.
Ornamented Brass Plating and Tipped	No. 2509.	42/-	45/-	48/-	54/- per dozen.

EXTRA SMALL EBONY LEVEL.

Ornamented Brass Plating and Tipped.

						If with Protecting Slides for Glass Tube.				
	8in.	9in.	10in.	12in.			8in.	9in.	10in.	12in.
No. 2512.	34/-	40/-	46/-	56/- per dozen.		No. 2513.	43/-	49/-	55/-	65/- per dozen.

Warranted Plumb and Spirit Levels,

WITH BEST PROVED TUBES.   FRENCH POLISHED.

Half size Drawings.

**BRASS PLATED
PLUMB AND LEVEL.
No. 2520.**

	8	9	10	12	14	16	18	20	inches
Extra Best Brass Plated Plumb and Level No. 2520.	30/-	34/-	38/-	44/-	54/-	66/-	78/-	90/-	per doz.
Brass Plated Plumb and Level No. 2519.	23/-	26/-	29/-	34/-	40/-	—	—	—	,,

**BRASS PLATED LEVEL
with FIELD SIGHT.
No. 2521.**

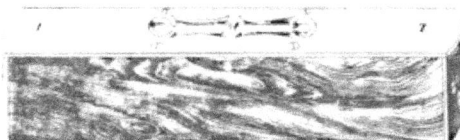

	8	9	10	12	14	inches
Extra Best Brass Plated Level and Field Sight No. 2521.	36/-	41/-	46/-	55/-	64/-	per dozen.
Brass Plated Level and Field Sight No. 2519.	27/-	31/-	34/-	40/-	48/-	,,

**ROSEWOOD
PLUMB & LEVEL,
FANCY BRASS PLATED.**

	8	9	10	12	14	inches
No. 2516.	40/-	43/-	46/-	52/-	60/-	per dozen.

HALF SIZE DRAWINGS.

Warranted Plumb and Spirit Levels,

WITH BEST PROVED TUBES.   FRENCH POLISHED.

Half size Drawings.

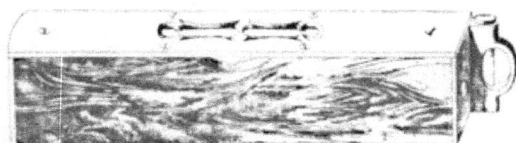

BRASS PLATED PLUMB & LEVEL, with Field Sight.

No. 2522.	8	9	10	12	14	inches.
	46/-	50/-	55/-	64/-	72/-	per dozen.

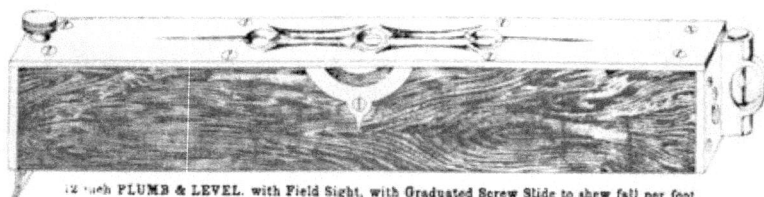

12 inch PLUMB & LEVEL, with Field Sight, with Graduated Screw Slide to shew fall per foot.

No. 2543.   8/6 each

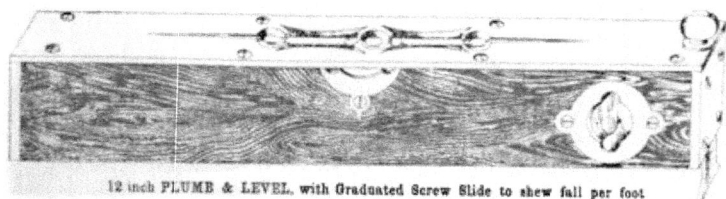

12 inch PLUMB & LEVEL, with Graduated Screw Slide to shew fall per foot

No. 2544.   8/- each.

Warranted Spirit Levels.

WITH BEST PROVED TUBES

Half size Drawings.

BRASS ADJUSTING LEVEL,
In neat Case.

		4	5	6	7	8	9	10	12	14	inches
No.	2524	18/6	23/-	28/-	33/-	37/-	42/-	—	—	—	per dozen.
If extra strong	2525	—	—	35/-	41/-	46/-	52/-	58/-	70/-	82/-	

BRASS ADJUSTING LEVEL,
with Revolving Tube Protector,
in neat Case.

		6	7	8	9	10	12	14	inches
No.	2526	35/-	41/-	46/-	52/-	58/-	—	—	per dozen
If extra strong	2527	40/-	47/-	54/-	66/-	72/-	90/-	108/-	

SQUARE BRASS LEVEL

		6	7	8	9	10	12	14	inches
No.	2530	20/-	24/-	27/-	31/-	35/-	42/-	66/-	per dozen

SQUARE BRASS LEVEL,
Raised Top and Field Sight.

		6	7	8	9	10	12	14	inches
No.	2523	48/-	56/-	64/-	72/-	80/-	96/-	120/-	per dozen

IRON LEVEL,
with Brass Top

		8	9	10	12	inches
No.	2531	16/-	20/-	24/-	32/-	per dozen
If all Brass	2532	30/-	34/-	40/-	52/-	

Warranted Spirit Levels,

WITH BEST PROVED TUBES.

Half size Drawings.

RABONES' SUPERIOR BRIGHT IRON LEVEL, Brass Top.
To Screw on Joiners' Square or Rule.

No. 2535.   9/- per dozen.

IRON LEVEL, Black Japanned.
To Screw on Joiners' Square or Rule.

No. 2534.   7/- per dozen.

SMALL BRASS LEVEL,
In Boxwood Case.

2½ inch Level.   No. 2536.   11/6 per dozen.
4 inch Level.   „ 2537.   20/-   „

Superior Strong Iron Level.

with Screw Adjustment and Scale, for shewing
inclination per yard,
especially adapted for
Gas and Water Works.

No. 1375.   9 inch, 6/6 each.   12 inch, 11/- each.

Masons' Boxwood Rule and Plumb Level.

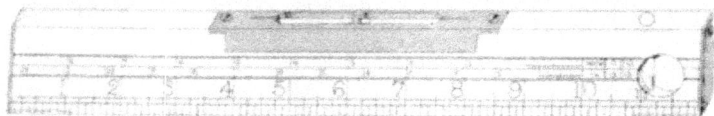

No. 2540.   12 inch, 33/- per doz.   18 inch, 43/-   24 inch, 58/- per doz.

Masons' Boxwood Rule Level.

No. 2538.   12 inch 25/- per dozen.

JOHN RABONE & SONS,
ENGINE DIVIDED STEEL RULES.

These Rules are made of best quality steel, well hardened and tempered ; are reliable straight edges, and are Engine divided with unvarying accuracy.

They are made with one rounded end, and with hole for hanging up, but may be had with both ends square if so ordered, at same prices.

The 4 inch and 6 inch Rules are ⅝ inch wide × 22 W.G. thick. The 1 foot Rules are 1¼ inch wide × 19 W.G. thick.

If Nickel Plated, 1 foot, 6/- per doz. extra subject.

10/- per doz.
No. 13. 4 inch.

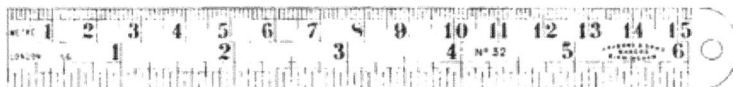

No. 32. 6 inch 12/- per doz.

No. 11. 1 foot. 15/- per doz.

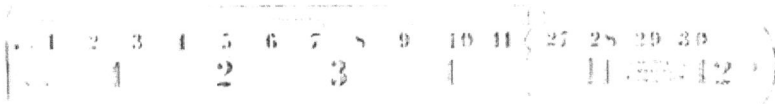

FRONT OF RULE No. 42.

BACK OF RULE No. 42. 1 foot. 30/- per doz.

In ordering these Rules from the following List, it is sufficient to quote the number of Rule and length required thus—No. 10, 12 inch, or No. 10, 4 inch.

The numbers under columns marked "Top Edge," "Bottom Edge," are the subdivisions of inches into which the Rule is marked.

EXAMPLE.—Rule No. 14 is marked on Top Edge, 3 inches into 20ths, 1 inch into 50ths, 1 inch into 100ths, and remaining 7 inches into 10ths ; and on the Bottom Edge, 3 inches into 32nds, 1 inch into 64ths, and remaining 8 inches into 16ths.

Any other measures or markings not in the following list, can be made to order at same prices.

JOHN RABONE & SONS,
ENGINE DIVIDED STEEL RULES,

WARRANTED CORRECT.

No. of Rule.	Sub-Divisions of Inches into which the different Edges of the Rules are Marked.				PRICE PER DOZEN.		
	FRONT OF RULE.		BACK OF RULE.		4-Inch Long.	8-Inch Long.	1-Foot Long.
	TOP EDGE.	BOTTOM EDGE.	TOP EDGE.	BOTTOM EDGE.			
	LONDON marked on two edges.						
10	8ths.	16ths.			8/-	9/-	12/-
11	16ths.	32nds. 64ths. 8ths.			10/-	11/-	15/-
12	10ths.	16ths.			8/-	9/-	12/-
13	20ths. 50ths. 10ths.	32nds. 64ths. 16ths.			10/-	11/-	15/-
14	20ths. 50ths. 100ths. 10ths.	32nds. 64ths. 16ths.			15/-	16/-	20/
15	12ths.	16ths.			8/-	9/-	12/-
16	24ths. 48ths. 12ths.	32nds. 64ths. 16ths.			10/-	11/-	15/-
17	24ths. 48ths. 96ths. 12ths.	32nds. 64ths. 16ths.			15/-	16/-	20/-
	LONDON MEASURE marked on four edges.						
24	12ths.	16ths.	10ths.	8ths.			18/-
25	16ths.	32nds. 64ths. 8ths.	8ths.	16ths.			20/-
26	24ths. 48ths. 12ths.	32nds. 64ths. 8ths.	20ths. 50ths. 10ths.	16ths.			22/
27	24ths. 48ths. 96ths. 12ths.	32nds. 64ths. 16ths.	20ths. 50ths. 100ths. 10ths.	16ths.			24/-
	LONDON & METRE, marked on two edges.						
	METRE.	*LONDON.*					
31	Millimetres.	8ths.			9/-	10/-	14/-
32	Millimetres.	16ths.			10/-	12/-	16/
33	Millimetres.	10ths.					16/
34	Half Millimetres and Millimetres.	32nds. 64ths. 16ths.			12/-	14/-	18/
35	" " "	20ths. 50ths. 10ths.			12/-	14/-	18/-
36	" " "	20ths. 50ths. 100ths. 10ths.					22/-
	LONDON & METRE, marked on four edges.						
	METRE.	*LONDON.*	*LONDON.*	*LONDON.*			
40	Millimetres.	16ths.	10ths.	12ths.	16/-	18/-	21/-
41	Half Millimetres and Millimetres.	32nds. 64ths. 16ths.	20ths. 50ths. 10ths.	24ths. 48ths. 12ths.	18/-	21/-	36/
42	" " "	" " "	20ths. 50ths. 100ths. 10ths.	24ths. 48ths. 96ths. 12ths.			30/

For Drawings and Descriptions of these Rules see opposite page.

The Numbers in most usual demand are 10, 11, 13, 14, 25, 32, 34, 42.

For these Rules marked with Foreign Measures, see pages, 42 to 47.

JOHN RABONE & SONS,
ETCHED STEEL RULES FOR SMITHS, &c.

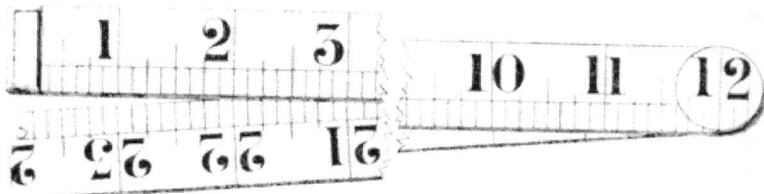

Flexible 2-feet 2-fold STEEL RULE, Spring Button Joint and Brass Bits at end.
No. 1291. 15/- per doz.

If without stop in Joint and Brass Bits.
No. 1312. 12/- per dozen.

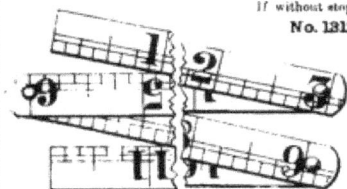

Very thin and flexible STEEL RULE,
to fold to 3 inches.
No. 1296, *see List below.*

Very thin and flexible STEEL RULE,
to fold to 4 inches.
No. 1297, *see List below.*

These Steel Rules are made of best Hardened and Tempered Steel, and are etched on both sides.
May be had marked with any foreign measures, or with two measures at same prices.

No. of Rule.		1-foot.	2-feet.	3-feet.	½ metre.	1 metre.	½ Ar-chine.	1 Ar-chine.
1296	¼ inch wide, to fold into 3 inches. G.S. rivets	5/-	10/-	15/-	8/	16/-	5/	10/-
1297	¼ inch wide, to fold into 4 inches. G.S. rivets	5/-	10/-	15/-	6/-	16/-	5/-	10/-
	Leather Cases for above, 2/6 per dos. extra.							
1295	½ inch wide, to fold into 6 inches. G.S. rivets	6/-	11/-	15/-	9/-	16/-	6/-	12/-
1294	½ inch wide, to fold into 6 inches, strong, with Button Joints	9/-	10/-	24/-	13/-	25/-	10/-	18/-
1291	2-feet 2-fold Spring Button Joint, and Brass Bits at ends, 15/- per dozen.							
1312	Same Rule as 1291, but without stop in Joint and Brass Bits, 12/- per dozen.							
1290	Same as 1291, but 1-foot long, without Joint, 6/- per dozen.							
1292	Straight Edge, marked on both sides, 1-foot, 18/-; 18-inch, 27/-, 24-inch, 36/- per dozen.							

PER DOZEN

The Rules in most usual demand are 1291, 1296, and 1297.

JOHN RABONE & SONS,
STEEL STRAIGHT EDGES.

No.	BRIGHT HARDENED STEEL STRAIGHT EDGE, one edge bevilled, and hole at end for hanging up	12	18	24	30	36	42	48	54	60	inches
1298	1½ inch wide × 14 W G thick	2/-	3/	4/							each.
1299	1¾ inch wide × 13 W G thick				5/6	6/9	8/-				
1300	2 inch wide × 12 W G thick							10/-	11/3	12/6	

The above may be had Nickel Plated at 6d. per dozen square inches extra.

SHOEMAKERS' STEEL STRAIGHT EDGE.

1810   1½ inch wide × 12 W.G. thick, marked inches in 8ths one side and Shoe sizes other side.

18 inch, 30/- per dozen   24 inch, 40/- per dozen.

STEEL COUNTER MEASURE, FOR SCREWING TO COUNTER.

1311   3 feet long, 1¾ inch wide × 16 W.G. thick, marked inches in ½ and Nails, and parts of yard.

24/- per dozen.

For Brass Counter Measures see Page 19.

Rabones' Patent Spring Measuring Tapes.

Packed in Half Dozens in Paper Boxes.

MARKED WITH ONE OR TWO MEASURES TO ORDER.

Full size Drawings.

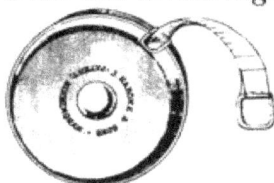

This article is the best and cheapest Spring Measure yet introduced. The Case has rounded edges, is highly finished, and Nickel Plated.

The Button sunk in the centre of the Case forms the Stop, which being pressed allows the tape to close into the case.

	3 feet.	6 feet.
No. 298.	14/-	19/- per dozen.

The Tape is carefully prepared and marked with Indelible Ink and is fastened on the ring with a Plated Mount.

The mouth of the case is framed to prevent the Tape wearing.

Nickel Plated Stop Case as above, with accurately marked Flexible. **STEEL TAPE.**

	3 feet.	6 feet.
No. 299.	21/-	36/- per dozen.

Nickel Plated Case as above, but without Stop.
LINEN TAPE.

	3 feet.	6 feet.
No. 300.	10/-	15/- per dozen.

Supplied with Foreign Measures at same prices.

FULL SIZE DRAWINGS.

Spring Measuring Tapes.

Packed in Quarter Dozens in Paper Boxes.

WITH FINE LINEN TAPES.   WITH ONE OR TWO MEASURES TO ORDER.

Full size Drawings.

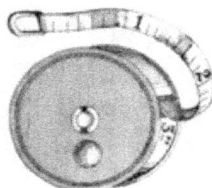

No.		3	4	5	6	9	12	18	feet.
302.	Brass Case Spring Stop ..	20/-	22/-	24/-	26/-	36/-	42/-	72/-	per doz.
303.	German Silver Case, Spring Stop	26/-	29/-	32/-	36/-	48/-	60/-	90/-	,,
330.	Brass Case, Spring Stop ..			24 feet, 9/- each.			33 feet, 11/- each.		
331.	German Silver Case, Spring Stop			,, 10/6 ,,			,, 13/- ,,		

Spring Measuring Tapes.
WITH
Flexible Steel Tapes.

WITH ONE OR TWO MEASURES TO ORDER.

No.		3	4	5	6	9	12	18	feet.
322.	Brass Case, Spring Stop ..	30/-	36/-	40/-	46/-	62/-	72/-	102/-	per doz.
323.	German Silver Case, Spring Stop	36/-	42/-	48/-	54/-	72/-	90/-	120/-	,,

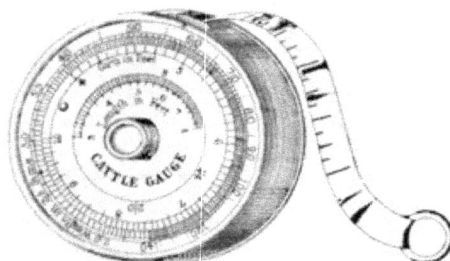

SPRING MEASURING TAPE.

12 feet long,

Marked English feet, inches, and hands, and

CATTLE GAUGE,

For ascertaining weight of Cattle by measure,

including full directions for use.

No.
340.   Brass Case, Spring Stop, Linen Tape, 7/- each.
341.   ditto   ditto   Steel Tape, 9/6 each.

Spring Measuring Tapes with Stops.

Much esteemed in Countries where several Measures are in use.

Full size Drawings.

No.		3	4	5	6	feet
	WITH FOUR MEASURES, two on each side.					per dozen
351.	Linen Tape, Brass Case ...	29/-	32/-	35/-	38/-	"
353.	„ German Silver Case....	34/-	38/-	42/-	45/-	"
355.	Steel Tape, Brass Case ...	36/-	42/-	48/-	56/-	"
357.	„ German Silver Case....	42/-	48/-	56/-	63/-	"
	WITH SIX MEASURES, three on each side.					
359.	Linen Tape, Brass Case ...	33/-	36/-	40/-	43/-	"
361.	„ German Silver Case....	40/-	43/-	47/-	50/-	"
363.	Steel Tape, Brass Case ...	42/-	48/-	56/-	69/-	"
365.	„ German Silver Case....	46/-	54/-	63/-	72/-	"
	WITH THREE MEASURES, on one side, and feet and yards of various countries on the other.					
367.	Linen Tape, Brass Case ..	32/-	36/-	40/-	44/-	"
369.	„ German Silver Case...	38/-	44/-	48/-	54/-	"
371.	Steel Tape, Brass Case ...	42/-	48/-	56/-	69/-	"
373.	„ German Silver Case...	46/-	54/-	63/-	72/-	"
	WITH FOUR MEASURES, on one side, and feet and yards of various countries on the other.					
375.	Linen Tape, Brass Case ...	35/-	40/-	45/-	50/-	"
377.	„ German Silver Case...	41/-	48/-	53/-	60/-	"

Wind-up Measuring Tapes, with Metallic Wired Tape.

These Tapes are specially made of the best fine Linen with **METALLIC WIRES** woven in the Tape and are then prepared, and marked with Indelible ink by special machinery with greatest accuracy. As supplied for Government Orders and the Admiralty.

Full size Drawing.
OF 66 FEET TAPE.

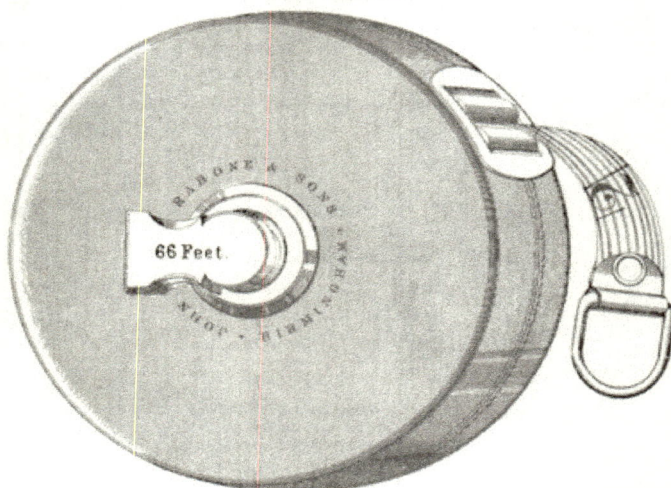

66 Feet.

MARKED ENGLISH FEET ON ONE SIDE, AND LINKS AND POLES ON THE OTHER SIDE, OR WITH ONE MEASURE.

WITH METALLIC WIRED BEST LINEN TAPE,		24 feet.	33 feet or 10 metres	40 feet.	50 feet or 15 metres	66 feet or 20 metres	75 feet.		100 feet or 25 metres	30 metres	40 metres	50 metres	
No.	⅜ inch wide.												
400.	Leather Case, Folding Handle	4/3	5/-	5/6	6/2	7/-	7/9		8/4	9/9	14/6	18/-	each.
401.	„ „ Flush Handle...	4/9	5/6	6/-	6/8	7/9	8/6		9/1	10/9	16/-	19/6	„
404.	Tapes only for the above (without Case) ...	1/11	2/6	3/-	3/5	4/-	1/6		5/-	6/6	—	—	„

If Marked on both sides of the Tape.

WITH METALLIC WIRED BEST LINEN TAPE,		24 feet.	33 feet or 10 metres	40 feet.	50 feet or 15 metres	66 feet or 20 metres	75 feet.		100 feet or 25 metres	30 metres	40 metres	50 metres	
No.	⅜ inch wide.												
400.	Leather Case, Folding Handle	4/6	5/3	5/9	6/6	7/6	8/3		8/11	10/6	15/3	19/-	each.
401.	„ „ Flush Handle...	5/-	5/9	6/3	7/-	8/3	9/-		9/8	11/6	16/9	20/6	„
404.	Tapes only for the above (without Case) ...	2/2	2/9	3/3	3/9	4/6	5/-		5/7	7/3	-	—	„

ANY FOREIGN MEASURES TO ORDER.

Wind-up Measuring Tapes,

WITH

Fine Linen Tapes.

These Tapes are made of the best fine Linen, carefully prepared, marked in Indelible ink with the greatest accuracy, by special Machinery.

Full size Drawing.

OF 66 FEET TAPE.

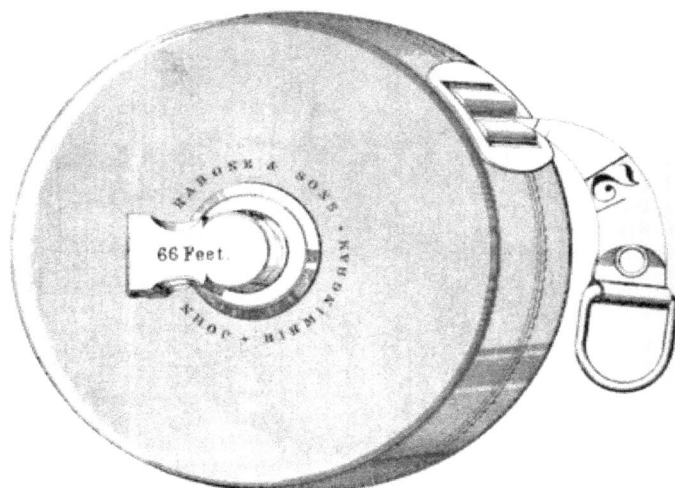

MARKED ENGLISH FEET AND INCHES ON ONE SIDE, AND LINKS AND POLES ON THE OTHER, OR WITH ONE MEASURE.

WITH BEST LINEN TAPE, No. ½ inch wide.	34 feet.	33 feet or 10 metres.	40 feet.	50 feet or 15 metres.	66 feet or 20 metres.	75 feet.	35 metres.	100 feet or 30 metres.	
405. Leather Case, Folding Handle	3/3	3/9	4/3	4/11	5/6	6/-	6/4	7/3	each.
406. ,, ,, Flush Handle	3/9	4/3	4/9	5/5	6/-	6/9	7/2	8/3	,,
408. Tapes only for the above (without Cases)	11d.	1/3	1/8	2/-	2/6	2/10	3/1	3/9	,,

If Marked on both sides of the Tape.

WITH BEST LINEN TAPE, No. ½ inch wide.	34 feet.	33 feet or 10 metres.	40 feet.	50 feet or 15 metres.	66 feet or 20 metres.	75 feet.	25 metres.	100 feet or 30 metres.	
405. Leather Case, Folding Handle	3/6	4/-	4/6	5/3	6/-	6/6	6/11	8/-	each.
406. ,, ,, Flush Handle	4/-	4/6	5/-	5/9	6/6	7/3	7/9	9/-	,,
409. Tapes only for the above (without Cases)	1/2	1/6	1/11	2/4	3/-	3/4	3/8	4/6	,,

ANY FOREIGN MEASURES TO ORDER.

Wind-up Measuring Tapes,
WITH
Linen Tapes—*Continued.*

Full size Drawing.
OF 66 FEET TAPE.

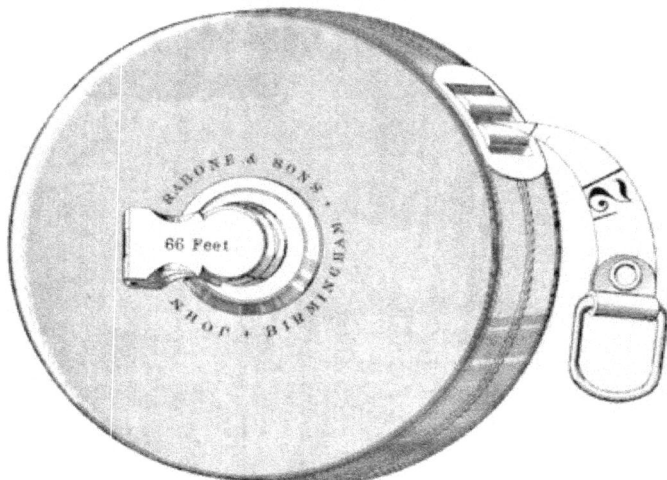

MARKED ENGLISH FEET AND INCHES ON ONE SIDE, AND LINKS AND POLES ON THE OTHER, OR MARKED ONE SIDE ONLY.

No.	WITH LINEN TAPE. ½ inch wide.	24 feet.	33 feet or 10 metres.	40 feet.	50 feet or 15 metres.	66 feet or 20 metres.	75 feet.	25 metres.	100 feet or 30 metres.	
410.	Leather Case, Folding Handle	2/10	3/2	3/10	4/3	4/8	5/2	5/7	6/3	each.
411.	,, ,, Flush Handle	3/4	3/8	4/4	4/9	5/5	5/11	6/4	7/3	,,
414.	Tapes only for the above (without Cases)	10d.	1/2	1/5	1/9	2/5	2/8	2/11	3/3	,,

If Marked on both sides of the Tape.

No.	WITH LINEN TAPE. ½ inch wide.	24 feet.	33 feet or 10 metres.	40 feet.	50 feet or 15 metres.	66 feet or 20 metres.	75 feet.	25 metres.	100 feet or 30 metres.	
410.	Leather Case, Folding Handle	3/–	3/4	4/–	4/6	5/–	5/6	6/–	6/9	each.
411.	,, ,, Flush Handle	3/6	3/10	4/6	5/–	5/9	6/3	6/9	7/9	,,
414.	Tapes only for the above (without Cases)	1/–	1/4	1/7	2/–	2/9	3/–	3/4	3/9	,,

ANY FOREIGN MEASURES TO ORDER.

Wind-up Measuring Tapes,
WITH
Steel Tapes.

Full size Drawing.
OF 66 FEET TAPE.

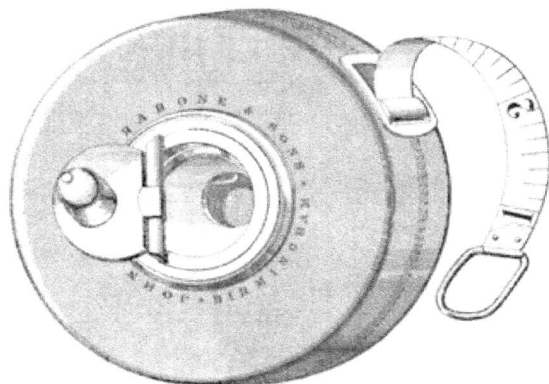

STEEL MEASURING TAPES have not hitherto been so widely known and used as their reliability, and freedom from either shrinking or stretching, would entitle them to be. For the Surveyor, they are the most convenient, portable, and trustworthy measures of long lengths. They are accurately marked, and are superior to Chains, as they never alter their length, nor require revision as Chains do. They are also less bulky than the Metallic Wired Tapes, and are considerably lighter.

The weight of the 66 feet Steel Tape with case (No. 415) is only 13 ounces.

MARKED ENGLISH FEET AND INCHES ON ONE SIDE, AND LINKS AND POLES ON THE OTHER, OR MARKED ONE SIDE ONLY.

No.	WITH STEEL TAPE, ¾ inch wide.	24 feet	33 feet or 10 metres	40 feet	50 feet or 15 metres	66 feet or 20 metres	75 feet	85 metres	100 feet or 30 metres	
415.	Leather Case, Flush Handle	10/-	12/-	14/-	17/-	21/-	24/-	27/-	30/-	each.
417.	Tapes only for the above (without Cases)	7/-	9/-	11/-	13/-	17/-	20/-	22/-	27/-	,,

If Marked on both sides of the Tape.

No.	WITH STEEL TAPE, ¾ inch wide.	24 feet	33 feet or 10 metres	40 feet	50 feet or 15 metres	66 feet or 20 metres	75 feet	25 metres	100 feet or 30 metres	
415.	Leather Case, Flush Handle	12/-	15/-	17/-	20/-	25/-	30/-	33/-	36/	each.
417.	Tapes only for the above (without Cases)	8/-	11/-	13/-	16/-	21/-	24/-	27/-	32/-	,,

ANY FOREIGN MEASURES TO ORDER.

Wind-up Measuring Tapes,

WITH

Steel Tapes—*Continued.*

MARKED ENGLISH FEET AND INCHES ON ONE SIDE, AND LINKS AND POLES ON THE OTHER,
OR MARKED ONE SIDE ONLY.

No.	WITH STEEL TAPE. ½ inch wide	24 feet.	33 feet or 10 metres.	40 feet.	50 feet or 15 metres.	66 feet or 20 metres.	75 feet.	25 metres.	100 feet or 30 metres.	
418.	Leather Case, Flush Handle ...	13/-	15/-	18/-	21/-	27/-	30/-	32/-	38/-	each.
420.	Tapes only for the above (without Cases)	8/-	11/-	13/-	16/-	21/-	24/-	27/-	32/-	,,
	WITH STEEL TAPE. ⅝ inch wide.									
421.	Leather Case, Flush Handle .	15/-	18/-	21/-	25/-	32/-	35/-	38/-	44/-	,,
423.	Tapes only for the above (without Cases)	10/-	13/-	16/-	19/-	25/-	29/-	31/-	38/-	,,
	WITH STEEL TAPE. ¾ inch wide.									
424.	Leather Case, Flush Handle ...	17/-	20/-	24/-	28/-	36/-	40/-	43/-	50/-	,,
426.	Tapes only for the above (without Cases)	11/-	15/-	17/-	21/-	29/-	33/-	36/-	44/-	,,

If Marked on both sides of the Tape.

No.	WITH STEEL TAPE, ½ inch wide	24 feet.	33 feet or 10 metres.	40 feet.	50 feet or 15 metres.	66 feet or 20 metres.	75 feet.	25 metres.	100 feet or 30 metres.	
418.	Leather Case, Flush Handle ..	15/-	18/-	21/-	25/-	33/-	36/-	39/-	46/-	each.
420.	Tapes only for the above (without Cases)	10/-	13/-	16/-	20/-	27/-	30/-	33/-	40/-	,,
	WITH STEEL TAPE, ⅝ inch wide.									
421.	Leather Case, Flush Handle ...	17/-	21/-	25/-	30/-	38/-	42/-	46/-	54/-	,,
423.	Tapes only for the above (without Cases)	12/-	16/-	19/-	24/-	31/-	36/-	39/-	48/-	,,
	WITH STEEL TAPE, ¾ inch wide.									
424.	Leather Case, Flush Handle ...	20/-	24/-	28/-	34/-	44/-	48/-	52/-	62/-	,,
426.	Tapes only for the above (without Cases)	14/-	19/-	22/-	27/-	37/-	41/-	45/-	56/-	,,

Marked on both sides of the Tape.

No.	WITH STEEL TAPE, ⅜ inch wide	6 feet.	9 feet.	12 feet.	15 feet.	18 feet.	24 feet.	33 feet.	
427.	Brass Case, Flush Handle	5/6	6/6	8/-	10/-	11/-	13/-	16/-	each.
428.	German Silver Case, Flush Handle ...	6/-	7/-	8/6	11/-	12/-	15/-	18/-	,,

ANY FOREIGN MEASURES TO ORDER.

TIMBER GIRTHING TAPES, TAILORS' TAPES, AND SHOEMAKERS' TAPES.

TIMBER GIRTHING TAPES, WITH RING AT END.

No.		M	4	5	6	7	8	9	10	11	12 feet
450	½-inch LINEN TAPE. Girth one side, Inches other side	2/3	2/6	3/-	3/6	4/-	4/6	5/3	5/9	6/6	7/- per dozen
452	½-inch BEST LINEN TAPE. Girth one side, Inches other side	2/6	3/-	3/6	4/-	4/9	5/3	6/-	6/9	7/6	8/- ,,
454	½-inch METALLIC WIRED TAPE. Girth one side, Inches other side	3/-	3/9	4/6	5/-	6/-	6/9	7/6	8/9	9/6	10/- ,,
456	½-inch STEEL TAPE. Girth one side, Inches other side	12/-	14/6	17/-	20/-	22/6	25/-	27/6	30/-	38/-	36/- ,,
458	½-inch STEEL TAPE. Girth one side, Inches other side	16/-	18/-	21/-	24/-	27/-	30/-	34/-	37/-	40/-	43/- ,,
460	½-inch STEEL TAPE. Girth one side, Inches other side	18/-	21/6	25/6	29/-	32/6	36/-	40/-	44/-	48/-	51/- ,,
462	½-inch STEEL TAPE Girth one side, Inches other side	21/-	25/-	29/-	33/-	39/-	42/-	46/-	51/-	55/-	59/- ,,

These Tapes may be had marked girth both sides, if required, at same price.

SHOEMAKERS' TAPES.

Marked 24 inches in N⁹ᵗ⁹ one side, and shoe sizes on other side.

No.		
465	½-inch Linen Tape	10/- per gross.
466	½-inch Linen Tape	11/- per gross.
467	½-inch Metallic Wired Tape	15/- per gross.

TAILORS' TAPES,
60 inches long.

Marked any foreign measures at same prices.

	Marked on one side.	Marked on both sides.
½-inch Tape	No. 470. 10/- per gross.	No. 471. 14/- per gross.
½-inch Linen Tape	No. 472. 14/- ,,	No. 473. 17/- ,,
½-inch Linen Tape	No. 474. 17/- ,,	No. 475. 20/- ,,
½-inch Metallic Wired Tape	No. 476. 21/- ,,	No. 477. 24/- ,,
½-inch Steel Tape, in Morocco case		18/- per dozen.

TAILORS' GRADUATING TAPES.
No. 478. 2/- per set.